WORKE

FOR

The Lives We Actually Have: 100

Blessings for Imperfect Days

(A Guild to Kate Bowler, Jessica Richie's Book)

Jeffery Clawson

THE COPYRIGHT OF THIS BOOK BELONGS TO JEFFERY CLAWSON. NO PART OF IT MAY BE REPRODUCED WITHOUT THE AUTHOR'S PERMISSION.

TABLE OF CONTENTS

Chapter 1
God promises us of a long life

Chapter 2
God's commitments to longevity

Chapter 3
Reclaiming lost blessings

Chapter 4
The more you give, the more blessings you receive

Chapter 5
Spiritual blessings we obtained from God

Chapter 6
Pleasing God in your daily prayers

CHAPTER 1

GOD PROMISES US OF A LONG LIFE.

God promises us of a long life. God has blessed us with long lives. God desires for you to live a full and fruitful life.

We need to be aware of the fact that we have power over how long we spend on earth.

Satan wants to give you a short life filled with danger, whereas God wants to give you a long life filled with abundance. Why does Satan want you to die, but God wants you to live?

You are in God's plans. He has tasks for you to complete that will benefit His kingdom and Him. He wants you to lead a life that draws people to you and inspires them to want to live similarly. Prosperity, serenity, and wealth in all things are what He wants for people who follow Him.

The devil wants to shorten your life, on the other hand. Satan is aware that one Spirit-filled Believer who is walking in all that God has for them might severely damage his dominion.

Jesus is aware that a believer who has a long life of good health and affluence will draw people to the Kingdom of God. Satan despises God and would do whatever to present the Kingdom of God in a detestable light.

Satan is the master of trickery. Satan manipulates us by persuading us to disobey, causing us to miss out on God's blessing of long life.

According to Proverbs 3:1–2, if we obey His rules and do not neglect His law, God will lengthen our days and prolong our lives. We reduce the number of days we have on this planet if we repeatedly disobey God's commands and don't repent. We restrict our time here on earth if our hearts are not fixed on obeying His rules.

Our life on earth will be prolonged if we honor our parents, according to Ephesians 6:2–3. Satan wants to destroy the family for a number of reasons, including this. Our lives are shortened by rebellion, domestic strife, and parental disgrace.

Indeed, the purpose of the thief's visit is to steal, kill, and destroy. We have to realize that he is out to destroy us, not anyone else. A Christian bears witness to God's glory every day that he lives on this planet in all that God has made him.

According to the Bible, "My son, do not forget my law, but let your heart maintain my precepts; for length of days and long life and tranquility they will add to you" (Prov. 3:1-2).

One other passage to bear in mind is this one: "Respect your father and your mother," which is the first commandment and has the blessing: "that it may go well with you and you may live a long time in the earth" (Eph. 6:2-3).

We should seek out God's Word, heed His instructions, and make every effort to extend our days. We honor Jesus by living in the fullness of God and His Word today.

Why is it important to pray for a long life?

1. That is God's strategy

God intends for us to have long lives and avoid passing away too soon. The Bible is where we can find proof for this. God originally intended for us to live a long life and finish everything He has predestined for us to complete.

And I'll give you long, prosperous lives. (Exodus 23:26b NLT)

2. It is a covenantal right of ours.

As Jesus died and rose from the dead, death was overcome. According to the Bible, Jesus vanquished the devil, who possessed the power of death. Jesus freed us, His children, from the fear of death by doing this (Hebrews 2:14-15)

3. The devil wants to take our rights away from us.

The only way the devil can steal from us is by making us fearful. Like any other fear, the fear of death is paralyzing. Faith in God's promises liberates, but fear torments.

How does the Bible treat the subject of longevity?

Wonderful promises are found throughout the Bible. The application of the Bible's teachings is what produces outcomes; simply knowing what it says is not enough. Faith is developed in us as a result of reflecting on God's promises and learning the truth. No matter what is happening around us, clinging to the word of faith will free us from all anxiety and offer us hope that we won't pass away too soon.

CHAPTER 2

GOD'S COMMITMENTS TO LONGEVITY

We become closer to the Source of our life by focusing on Him because He is both the span of our days and the source of our life. We will draw from His life, extending our days, through Adoring Him and clinging to Him in faith. He can give us that life as long as we put our trust in Him and His promises of it.

According to Psalm 84:11–12, "Because the LORD God is a sun, bringing us health, and a shield, keeping us from disease. The LORD will grant grace and honor." He won't deny people who walk uprightly anything pleasant, not even a long life. The man who puts his trust in You, O LORD of hosts, is blessed! "

Bless the LORD, O my soul, and do not forget all His benefits. He is the one who pardons all your transgressions, heals all your illnesses, saves your life from destruction, crowns you with loving kindness and tender mercies, and fills your mouth with good things so that your youth is renewed like the eagle's (Psalm 103:2–5).

God's blessings are freedom from destruction (early death), healing from all illnesses, pardon for all sins, and the restoration of our youth (long-life). By recognizing them and giving God praise for them, we are to keep in mind ("forget not") all the blessings promised in the Bible. Consequently, we are to recite the gifts of healing and long life that God has promised and express our gratitude to Him by saying, "Thank You, Lord, for forgiving all my sins, for curing all my illnesses, and for renewing my youth like the eagle."

Proverbs 3:1,2 says, "My son, forsake not my rule; but let your heart observe my precepts; for length of days and long life and peace will they add unto you." This verse refers to both the quality and the duration of life. Shalom (peace) denotes blessed, flourishing days of wholeness. Long life and length of days refer to numerous days. In light of this, we can conclude that God desires for us to lead long, fulfilling lives. This is attainable if we would pay close attention to His Word.

Proverbs 3:13–18: "Blessed is the man who discovers knowledge and the man who obtains understanding; for her reapings are better than the reapings of silver, and her gain superior to pure gold. All the things you may want cannot compare to her since she is more valuable than rubies. Her right hand holds the number of days. Her left hand held wealth and prestige. Her pathways are all peaceful, and they are lovely ones. She is a TREE OF LIFE to those who grasp her, and those who hang onto her are happy.

God's Word contains His WISDOM. In this case, God is encouraging us to seek out and discover His wisdom by assuring us that if we do, she will grant us life and a long life. We may once more understand that His will for us is LONG LIFE.

Proverbs 4:10 says, "My son, receive My sayings; and (as a result) the years of your life shall be numerous." God desires us to live many years of life through receiving His Word.

Proverbs 10:10–11 "The beginning of wisdom is the fear of the LORD (respect and deference for His authority), and understanding is the knowledge of the Holy.

Your days will be multiplied by wisdom, and your years of life will lengthen "As you humble yourself before God and His Word, you will start to receive the wisdom that God wants you to receive, and this will help you live a longer life.

As stated in Proverbs 10:27, "The fear of the LORD prolongs days; but the years of the wicked shall be shortened." While sin inevitably results in death, God wants you to live as long as possible.

God said to Solomon in 1 Kings 3:14 that if he walked in His ways and obeyed His commands, "I will lengthen his days." God wants us to live a long life and makes the promise of long life, but it depends on us walking in His ways. We will get His Life if we are in close proximity to the Source of Life.

Exodus 20:12 says, "Honor your father and your mother, so that your days may be long in the land which the LORD your God is giving you." This commandment is so crucial that God included it in the list of the Ten Commandments that He inscribed on stone with His own finger! Having a pledge, it is the first Commandment. If we honor and respect our parents, he assures us, we will live a long time on this planet.

40 years later, God reiterated and strengthened the promise of long life from Exodus 20:12 in Deuteronomy 5:16: "Honor your father and your mother, as the LORD your God ordered you, that your days may be long, and that it may be well with you in the land which the LORD your God is giving you." He is now promising both a long life and a good one. Our days on earth won't only be long—they'll be many days—but also happy days, as in "it will be well with you."

Psalm 34:12,13: "Who is the person that loves life, and prolonged days, that he also can moreover see good days by offering us a key to achieving this: preventing our tongue from saying evil. "Keep your tongue from wickedness, and your lips from speaking falsehood," he says. He guarantees us a long life and many happy days if we control our speech.

My favorite is from Psalm 91, which is full of promises about how God will guard and preserve our lives if we put our trust in Him. God speaks directly in verses 14–16 to bring it to a close.

He will call on me and I will answer him: I will be with him in distress; I will deliver him, and I will honor him. WITH LONG LIFE SHALL I SATISFY HIM, and show (manifest to) him My salvation(preservation from death).

God promises in Psalm 91:16 that He will satisfy a man with long life if he dwells in the secret chamber of the Almighty and is covered by the shadow of His wings. God desires for us to experience complete satisfaction and to live out our entire life cycle without interruption. According to the Jerusalem Bible, God desires to do this for us: "I give them life, long and full, and show them how I may save." He wants us to be happy, so if 70 years isn't enough, we can keep going to 80, 90, 100, and even 120 until we are!

Long life is MANY DAYS, and since we will be satisfied with them, this indicates that they will also be GOOD DAYS during which we will keep our fundamental health and mental clarity. This so represents a promise of both quantity and quality of existence.

Obviously, our mortal bodies do not allow us to live eternally, yet

Instead of having a short life, we can live a life full with days.

Our understanding is greatly aided by KENNETH HAGIN's narrative. When he was 17 years old, he overcame paralysis and a fatal blood illness by following the advice in Mark 11:24: "So I say to you, whatever things you ask for (including healing), when you pray, believe that you receive them, and you will have them."

After being bedridden for some time, he was finally free to leave his bed and go to breakfast after obtaining his recovery. He returned to his bed after breakfast to rest because he was still weak, and not long after, a deep, unearthly voice could be heard in his head. It said:

What is your life? It's nothing more than a fleeting vapour, I tell you (James 4:14). Even though you have been healed, your assigned time has come because everyone has a finite lifespan (Hebrews 9:27). (Isaiah 38:1).

He assumed the speaker was God because the passages were from the Bible. In order to await death, he sat down. The devil can quote scripture, but he will twist, take it out of context, and apply it in a wrong way (something supernatural is not necessarily God).

He didn't even realize that statement was found in the Bible when the words "With long life will I satisfy him and show him My salvation" began to bubble up from deep inside.

Later, a second voice reappeared and repeated what it had said. Later, the words "With long life will I satisfy him and show him My salvation" began to bubble up from within.

And for the third time, he heard the deep voice. He asked: "Who said that?" The inner voice replied: "The 91st Psalm." He looked it up and read: "with Long life will I satisfy him." He reasoned: "Well, I'm only 17, I'm not satisfied yet. I'll be content with a long life, the Bible says," but then the opposite voice returned, saying:

That was an Old Testament blessing, thus the promise was made to the Jews, not the Church.

Hence, he made the decision to look up all the cross references to see if this promise was repeated in the New Testament so that we could be certain that it applied to us. He quickly discovered Ephesians 6:2, which reads, "Honor your father and mother (the first commandment with promise): that it may be good with you and that you may live a long time on the earth" (quoting from Exodus 20:12 and

Deuteronomy 5:16). This promise still holds true today because it is in the New Testament, which is obvious.

Additionally, in the New Testament, he discovered 1Peter 3:9, 10:

The Bible says, "You are called to inherit a blessing. For he who wishes life, and loves to see MANY GOOD DAYS, let him stop his lips from evil" (from Psalm 34:12-16). The blessing is ours to inherit (under the New Covenant). Whose blessing? MANY NICE DAYS' blessing!

He also understood that God never changes and that the New and Better Covenant we currently have with Israel is superior to the Old Covenant. He (Jesus) is also the Mediator of a better Covenant, which was founded on better promises, according to Hebrews 8:6. If the Old Covenant's promise of long life applied to us at this time, then it must do so now as well;

otherwise, the New Covenant would be inferior to the Old Covenant.

As soon as Kenneth Hagin realized this, he realized that the first voice was actually Satan speaking in the name of God, trying to convince him to give up and accept sickness and death as God's will. He stood up and said, "Devil, I'm not going to die today, tomorrow, next week, next year, I'm not going to die in five years, I'm not going to die in ten years, I'm not going to die in twenty years, I'm not going to die in thirty, forty, or even fifty years. I can be happy with an extended life." And it happened that he did live a long and fruitful life before going on to be with the Lord.

In the New Testament, the promises of long life are therefore not limited to the Old Testament but are also reiterated:

Likewise, God makes it plain that He wants us to live long lives with many good days, but this requires us to honor our parents. Ephesians 6:2,3 says, "Honor your father and mother (the first commandment with promise): That it may be well with you, and you may live long on the earth."

You are designated to receive a blessing, according to 1 Peter 3:9–10.

What gift are we supposed to receive? Continuing on,

You'll see that it is a blessing from a long and fulfilling life:

Because he or she should hold back their tongue from wickedness if they want to live and see many good days (from Psalm 34:12-16)

In John 10:10, Jesus declared that, despite the fact that the devil seeks to steal, kill, and destroy, he has come to give us abundant LIFE—life both here on earth and in heaven.

Through the blood of Jesus, God confirms to us that every promise is ours in Christ. However, we must know and receive (embrace) the promise for ourselves, adding our 'Amen' by confessing the promise as true for us. Then it will surely come to pass to the glory of God through us.

We need to know these promises so well that no one could ever talk us out of believing them. LONG LIFE is God's will for us. God has promised it to us in the New-Covenant in Christ. So let us believe and receive these promises now. We need to establish our faith in God now for a long and blessed life.

As we trust God daily for His abundant life to sustain us in good health, soundness of mind, and long life, we can see that this is God's will for us (John 10:10). In fact, Jesus took the curse of an early death for us in order that we might have the blessing of a long and full life (Galatians 3:13,14).

Let's look at a few of these priceless Pledges first.

-to strengthen our belief that living a long life is in God's will for us. Our faith is based on our knowledge of God's will. It is the time to put our trust in God's promises of healing and long life. Before you begin to receive these promises, don't wait until your body is in danger. By reflecting on these promises, you can immediately improve your overall health and resistance to disease.

By being aware of, holding fast to, and proclaiming these promises, we must right away strengthen our trust for wellbeing. Because Jesus taught that "Healing is the children's bread" (Matthew 15:26), we need to lay hold of God's supply of LIFE and HEALING for our bodies every day. We should pray, "Give us this day our daily bread (our daily healing)" every day (Matthew 6:11). In this way, we will be preparing ourselves to receive God's life and healing when we truly need them as well as to withstand illness and death when they come against us.

The Bible is replete of promises that demonstrate God's will for us is for us to live long and fruitful lives. God makes these promises to us so that our confidence will be strengthened and prepared to receive His blessing. He also outlines the actions we must take in order for these promises to come true.

Have a peek at a few of these priceless Promises:

God discloses His plan for us in Exodus 23:25–26: "You shall serve the Lord your God, and He will bless your bread and water; and I will remove disease from among you, and the (full) number of your days I will fulfil." His plan is to BLESS, and His blessing is health and long life. God prefers that our lives be fully lived as opposed to being brief.

Deuteronomy 11:18–21 states, "Therefore, you must lay up these words of mine in your heart and in your spirit, and bind them for a token upon your hand, and they shall be as frontlets between your eyes. When you sit at home, when you stroll down the street, when you lie down, and when you get up, you should mention them to your kids. We see that God wants both quantity and quality of life for His people, and that is why He commands you to write these things on your house's doorposts and on your gates so that your days and the days of your children can be multiplied in the land that the LORD promised to give it to them.

He want to lengthen our earthly days so that they resemble the days of heaven (days of love, joy and peace).

God's desire for us to live a long time must be obvious. (Deuteronomy 30:19, 20) I set before you LIFE and DEATH, blessing and cursing; therefore, choose LIFE so that both you and your descendants may LIVE; so that you may LOVE the LORD your God, so that you may follow His voice, so that you may CLING to Him, for HE IS YOUR LIFE and the LENGTH OF YOUR DAYS.

If we make the proper choice to choose LIFE, God wants us to have it and He makes it possible for us to have it (v19). This offer of LIFE (v. 20) demonstrates that LONG LIFE is His will for us because it plainly involves the Length OF DAYS. Also, He instructs us on how to select wisely and accept the long life He provides.

CHAPTER 3

RECLAIMING LOST BLESSINGS

According to the Bible, God has promised us as His children a number of blessings. Many people, nevertheless, never get to experience these blessings in their entirety. Regaining lost benefits enters our minds more and more as the year comes to a close. We must be aware of what to do in order to receive God's blessings for the coming year. We desire healthy bodies, prosperous finances, and successful relationships. Even though God gave us all of these things and more in His word, we find it difficult to hold onto them. We have put together a few keys to help you restore your lost blessings if you have reached this point.

God is not Santa Claus, who leaves you a gift every Christmas by coming down your chimney. He has more in store for you than Santa Claus or a genie combined. The Bible clearly establishes that God is the source of all things in a number of verses.

According to 2 Peter 1:3 and Ephesians 1:3, God is always prepared to reward us; in fact, He has already done so. According to both texts, God has already benefited us and is not going to do so. Why haven't we captured them if he has? We haven't made a decision yet, but it is straightforward.

The wealthiest guy in the world hands you a blank check. Input the amount you need, then withdraw the funds from the bank. You still have a ton of debt huge pay in addition to overdue obligations. You would remain struggling with money issues until you made the decision to cash the cheque at the bank.

As Christians, we aspire to benefits, but we must make the decision to take use of the advantages that are currently accessible to us.

Even if He has already written you a blank check, He won't fill it on your behalf; you must do it on your own.

You must comprehend and accept that God is not just the "bless-er," but also the "blessing" if you want to receive the blessings He promised. Because of this, He is the source of all good and flawless gifts (James 1:17). God has a "blessing plan" ready for you; He doesn't just wait for you to ask for blessings from Him.

Jesus Christ advised us to avoid praying ineffectively (Matthew 6:7). He wants us to pray deliberately and with clarity. The effectiveness of your prayers depends less on the number of words you use and more on how clearly you express your intentions.

How could you possibly meet with the Alpha and Omega without outlining your demands in detail? Indeed, we often act in this way unintentionally. We spend a lot of time praying, but we're not really clear what we want. Learn to ask for specific things and to be as honest as you can. You can't conceal anything from God, so don't be afraid to be open with Him.

As Christians, we want benefits, but we must make the conscious decision to draw upon the gifts that are already at hand. He has already written you a blank check, but He won't cash it for you; you must do it on your own.

According to Hebrews 11:6, we must approach God in confidence if we want to satisfy Him or get something from Him. The significance of faith in regaining benefits is emphasized in a number of additional biblical scriptures.

You need to continue studying the Bible if you believe that your faith is weak or nonexistent. According to Romans 10:17, hearing God's word causes our faith to grow. When the word plants the germ of our faith, prayer in the Holy Spirit nurtures and grows it (Jude 1:20).

You may boldly approach God's throne because of faith since you know He can grant your desires. It also gives you the confidence that God is listening to you and has already benefited you.

Giving gratitude is one of the most effective strategies to gaining access to God's gifts in your life. We should enter His gates with gratitude, according to Psalm 100:4. We are instructed to "enter with the password, 'Thank you!'" according to the Message translation of the same passage.

By expressing gratitude, you get unrestricted access to God's presence. It also enables you to see how much God has already done for you but you were unaware of. More than anything, it strengthens your trust because you know that if God could accomplish it in the past, He can certainly do it now.

We have all we need thanks to God's blessings. It is time to take these gifts back and start living them out. Use the aforementioned keys as the year comes to a close to unlock God's blessings over your life.

CHAPTER 4

THE MORE YOU GIVE, THE MORE BLESSINGS YOU RECEIVE

"In fact, becoming a spiritual conduit as opposed to a spiritual dead end can bring you more blessing in God's economy. God wants to use you to help others by working through you. Be used by God to contribute to and satisfy a need if you have the ability to do so (with your money, your time, or your support). God will give something back."

When we donate, we humble ourselves and make a gift that God accepts favorably. God wants to reward people who follow Him and work toward building His earthly kingdom! Let's now look at 10 particular reasons why giving is more fortunate than receiving. The Old Bible has far more instructions on who, when, and how much to give financially than the New Testament. Maybe the authors of the New

Testament simply felt that because God had given so much more to us in the New Testament—offering Himself up for death—that our giving would naturally and logically follow. Yet, in case we would overlook the connection, there are also very plain New Testament directives (e.g. 1 Corinthians 1:2). Following this command will make us happier since God's instructions are all meant to improve our lives.

Every act of submission acknowledges the existence of a greater power in our life, a Lord who is deserving of our respect and reverence. Certain directives may be very simple for us to follow depending on our temperament, personality, or situation. The areas where it is harder for us to obey due to our nature and circumstances are where our submission is truly put to the test. One of those areas is money for the majority of us. Our pocketbook is often the last fortress to submit to God's reign, and even when it does, it is swiftly rebuilt and resecured. If only we could keep in mind that Divine Sovereignty is the area of ultimate safety rather than posing a danger.

God is THE source of all good and ideal gifts (James 1:17). We are obligated to emulate His generosity as bearers of His image and to reflect His endlessly vast heart. The bigger the image we create of God's nature, the bigger our hearts (and hands) must be. What do others believe about God when they consider how you handle your finances?

The Gospel is centered on selfless sacrifice (John 3:16). Because of this, when the Apostle Paul wished to inspire the Corinthians to donate more, he referred to Christ and his life and work. For you are aware of the grace of our Lord Jesus Christ, who, while being wealthy, became poor for your benefit so that you may become rich by His poverty (2 Corinthians 2:9). You do have a lot of faith, love, etc., but you also need to have a lot of grace. We are flimsily and modestly teaching the Gospel when we offer painfully and sacrificially for the benefit of others.

Fear, the worry that if I give too much, I won't have enough for this or that, is the largest barrier to giving. By giving sacrificially, above and beyond what is convenient and pleasant, we demonstrate our faith and confidence that God will take care of our needs and those of our family. This is a case for faith rather than foolishness. Many Christians have experienced the thrill of tossing their breadcrumbs into the sea and seeing many loaves appear after several days (Ecclesiastes 11:1). When we follow God, it is such a delight to watch Him fulfill His promise of sustenance.

A joyful giver is loved by the Lord (2 Corinthians 2:7). The fact that His people are willingly extending their hearts and hands to meet the needs of His Church and, in fact, of all of His creation, makes Him happy. God continually honors and celebrates individuals who sacrificed of themselves and of their resources to gospel work via the apostle Paul (2 Corinthians 8:1). Nothing makes a Believer happier than knowing that her actions have brought joy to God, and joyful giving makes God joyful.

Many of us have made some kind of contribution to Apple. We have aided in the company's expansion from a garage operation to the global powerhouse it is today. And I'm glad about it because this is a business that has given the world a lot of good things. But consider the benefits of supporting the work of Christ's church. We support missionaries and clergy with wages. Resources for evangelism, discipleship, and outreach are being funded by us. The spiritual and eternal well-being of individuals from every country, race, clan, and language is our primary concern. Homes, relationships, nations, and even countless people' eternal fate are being changed by our money.

Giving encourages both God's work in us, our sanctification, as well as God's work through us. Giving money demands a lot of self-denial and self-crucifixion, particularly when it hurts us. Yet the more we give, the more God's mercy spreads in our hearts since giving weakens and even ruins our sinful and selfish nature. Money does indeed leave our pockets, but so does evil from our souls. And it's a lot, too. Really priceless.

It's very clear that Christians contribute a lot of money to their churches and Christian organizations, despite the commandment to keep our left hand from knowing what our right hand does. Even non-Christian onlookers have been astounded by how frequently Christians are very giving with their money. Even if they don't say it, they must be thinking it: "If people are giving out so much of their own money, then this must be the genuine thing. These people must really think this. To inspire individuals to give so freely, the God they love and serve must be extraordinarily strong.

Giving with the proper attitude is a kind of adoration. That is paying Him a praiseworthy homage. It is expressing. "You gave me everything, and this is just a little way for me to thank and appreciate you for all of your wonderful gifts. You know the heart that lays behind it, even if it's only a little fraction of what I really feel. What should I give the Lord in return for all of his favours to me, David sang in the song. (12 Psalms 116).

CHAPTER 5

SPIRITUAL BLESSINGS WE OBTAINED FROM GOD

Knowing that your life matters means you have been selected from the beginning of time. Natural selection did not happen by chance or produce you. Before He ever spoke, "Let there be light," God was already planning your future.

You are spotless and holy in Him. This indicates that despite your flaws, you are suitable to serve Him and to adore Him. It is not because of your own righteousness that God likes you when you come to Him; rather, it is because of the righteousness of Christ that has been credited or assigned to you.

You are in agape, or unwavering love, in Christ. It cannot be earned. You have an everlasting love in Christ today. Have you gotten it yet? Declare this confession right now: "Lord, I accept your unfailing love."

God has already decided to claim you as His own via Jesus. You are His son or daughter because He has chosen you. A member of His family, you are. Your father, he is. When parents decide to adopt a kid, they often go through a selection process to choose which children they would and won't take in. God had made up His mind to adopt you as one of His offspring a long time ago after going through His decision-making process.

You are not turned down. You're not a misfit. You are deserving of respect. You are welcomed by the universe's Creator via Christ. In Christ, you have experienced interpersonal reconciliation, and you now please God. Even if not all of your relationships are healthy at the moment, nothing stands between you and God because of Christ.

You were a slave to sin and death without Him. You were unable to escape it via purchase or work. Jesus' priceless blood served as the payment for your freedom. Jesus didn't have a master. Jesus already had freedom. Nonetheless, Jesus paid for your freedom.

You have ethically rejected God throughout your life. In your heart, you have willfully rebelled against His law. You have often disregarded His advice and believed yourself to be more knowledgeable. You have today's forgiveness in Christ.

"Unmerited favor" is what grace implies. The verb "to have in plenty" is abound. Your life is being lavished with undeserved favor through Christ in an abundance that will continue from now until the very end of time.

God has made known to us His remedy for a fallen world plagued by conflict, misery, and disease—a world marred by sin where good people experience evil things. He provided us with Christ, who served as the solution to every problem related to the human situation.

Heaven is described in Revelation 21:4 as having no more death, sorrow, or weeping, and God will wipe away every tear from their eyes. Because the earlier things are no longer there, there won't be any more suffering. A light in the night is God's truth. We have access to advice. We're not in the dark, either. We are aware of His good news and the way of life.

You now have access to the Holy Spirit Promise that was foretold by the prophets Isaiah, Ezekiel, Zechariah, Joel, John the Baptist, and Jesus! You may place all of your eggs in His calling over your life. An anchor, that is. A rock, that. Never will it be in vain.

You are very important to Him. God gives you back to Jesus as His inheritance in the same way that Christ reconciled you to Himself. In Christ, you have value because you represent God's righteousness. You are His prize for eternity, which He treasures.

According to Paul, His power is very tremendous toward those of you who believe. How much power does this have? The same force that resurrected Christ from the grave is at work here. That same force overcame sin, death, and hell. This same power is at work in your life right now via Christ!

CHAPTER 6

PLEASING GOD IN YOUR DAILY PRAYERS

Every brother and sister is aware that we may speak with God via prayer. We pray before and after meals, during meetings, on the Sabbath, and other occasions in addition to in the morning and evening. So just how should we pray if we want our requests to be heard by God and carried out according to His will? Every sibling should be aware of it. The solution to this question has already been revealed to us by the Lord Jesus. Together, let's look for this facet of the truth.

First: While praying, do not be self-righteous, maintain our position, and have a humble heart.

And he related this story to those who believed in themselves that they were righteous and hated others, according to Luke 18:9–14. One was a Pharisee and the other a publican, and both men entered the temple to worship. God, I thank you that I am not like other men who are extortionists, unjust, adulterers, or even like this publican, the Pharisee stood and prayed to himself. I donate tithes of whatever I own and observe two weekly fasts. Then the publican prayed, "God be gracious to me, a sinner," while standing some distance away and refusing to even raise his eyes to heaven. Since everyone who exalts themselves will be debased, and everyone who humbles themselves will be exalted, I can assure you that this guy returned home more justified than the other. It is clear from the parable told by the Lord Jesus that the Lord loved the prayer of the publican but despised that of the Pharisee. Because the Pharisee's prayer consisted of self-promotion and peacock play. The Pharisee, full of pretense and self-righteousness, estimated his own merits before God while looking down on the publican. God despised him because he had no awareness of his rank or position, had no godly conduct in front of God, and had already established himself in a position of equality with God. Yet the prayer of the publican was very different since he was really sorry, prayed before God humbly, and had a godly attitude because he understood he was a sinner with a humble identity. He truly asked God for forgiveness, and God graciously granted him compassion. I tell you, this man walked down to his home justified rather than the other, for everyone who exalts himself shall be abased, and he who humbles himself shall be exalted, the Lord Jesus remarked in reference to their differing views of God. If we want God to hear our prayers, we should not pray like the Pharisee but rather like the publican, positioning ourselves appropriately as a created person. As we pray in God's presence, we should have a pious attitude, respect God as God, regularly think on the wrongs we have done that are not pleasing to the Lord, and really repent and confess before God. We also must certainly avoid being complacent or cocky. Only in this manner can God hear our requests. In accordance with what Jehovah God previously said: "If my people, who are called by my name, should humble themselves, and pray, and seek my face, and turn from their wicked ways; then I will hear from heaven, and will forgive their sin, and I will heal their land. I'll be listening to the prayer being said here with my eyes wide and ears alert right now (2 Chronicles 7:14-15).

Second: Intercede for God Actually and Sincerely

The Lord Jesus once instructed His followers, "And when you pray, you must not be as the hypocrites are; for they love to stand in the synagogues and at the corners of the streets, praying, so they may be seen by mankind. They received their recompense, I assure you in truth. But you, when you pray, go into your closet and, after closing the door, pray to your Father in private; your Abba, who sees in secret, will reward you in public (Matthew 6:5-6). We might infer from the Lord Jesus' instruction to His followers that He detested the Pharisees' phony prayers. They deliberately wore really sorrowful expressions and appeared to pray for a long time so that everyone would know they were fasting and praying. The Jewish people wanted to seem to be the most devoted to God, so that others would respect and look up to them. Yet, in such prayers, they didn't have a true relationship with God; instead, they followed the procedures. God would not accept a prayer like that because it was dishonest to Him. God created everything. We should have a reverent attitude toward God and adore Him with all of our hearts when we pray to Him. If, like the Pharisee, we spend many hours each day praying but don't engage with God, instead only following religious rituals and laws, then God will see our prayers as a waste of time, a swindle, and will despise them. God is a Spirit, and those who worship him must do so in spirit and in truth, the Lord Jesus taught (John 4:24). Thus, when we pray, we should do it with a heart that reveres God, accept God's observations, and express to God the true feelings that are in our hearts. Our prayers can only delight God in this way.

Thirdly: Ask God to help you carry out his will.

According to Matthew 6:9–13, you should pray in the following way: "Our Father in heaven, hallowed be your name. God's kingdom come and His will be carried out on earth as it is in heaven. And keep us away from temptation while saving us from harm. God desires for more people to embrace His redemption and turn away from Satan's evil so that His will may be carried out on earth and the kingdom of Christ may come to pass. Therefore, rather than praying for ourselves, we should pray for the following: God's will to be accomplished on earth; the establishment of the kingdom of Christ on earth; the proclamation of the gospel; our ability to spread the gospel and serve as witnesses for God; and our ability to as quickly as possible become those who are after God's heart. God has heard and answered everyone of these petitions. Similar to how King David put his heart on building the temple for Jehovah God so that people may worship the Almighty there, the Old Testament of the Bible records this. He therefore became the one who delighted Jehovah God. A prayer like that was heard by God. After becoming king, Jehovah God revealed to Solomon in a dream that he had the power to make requests. But, Solomon chose to ask for wisdom to rule God's people rather than wealth or a long life. As a consequence, God provided him wealth and long life in addition to the knowledge he had previously requested. Our prayers will be heard by God if we love Him with all of our hearts, keep His will in mind, and ask that His kingdom come and that His will be done.

Last but not least': Pray to God with perseverance, resolve, and never give up.

According to Luke 18:1–8, "And he told a parable to them to this intent, that men ought continually to pray and not weary; Saying, There was in a city a judge who feared not God, nor looked upon man: There was a widow in that city, and she approached him and pleaded with him to get revenge on her enemy. He first refused, but afterwards changed his mind, saying, "Even if I do not fear God or heed man, I will get revenge on this widow because she bothers me, should her constant presence tire me out." Hear what the wicked judge said, the Lord commanded. And even if he has been patient with his own chosen, who cry out to him day and night, would God not get revenge? He will swiftly get revenge on them, I assure you. But will the Son of Man find trust on the world when he returns? Through the story of the Lord Jesus, we learn that we shouldn't put too much pressure on God to answer our prayers right away since He is a practical God and doesn't do miracles. According to His principles, He answers people's prayers in various ways. Sometimes, He examines our devotion to Him and our allegiance to others; other times, He cleanses our inner defilement. As a result, no matter what challenge we encounter in life or in service, we should, like the widow who begged the judge to exact revenge, have a heart of perseverance, constantly come to pray and seek before God, and wait for God's will to manifest itself to us without becoming discouraged. Similar to how the Israelites prayed and cried out to God nonstop to be delivered from hardships when they were being oppressed by Pharaoh in Egypt. Despite the fact that God did not immediately answer their prayers, they remained hopeful and continued to pray to God despite their lack of immediate success. To lead them out of Egypt and into the prosperous country of Canaan, God at last exalted Moses. As we face issues head-on and pray to God consistently while being active and unafraid, the Holy Spirit will enlighten and illuminate us so that we may witness God's magnificent actions.